HOW TO CREATE A CULTURE OF FULL ENGAGEMENT

QUICK START GUIDE
MARK MILLER & RANDY GRAVITT

Printed in the United States of America
Design and Layout by Lindsay Miller

Printing Information
Bennett Graphics
125 Royal Woods Court, Suite 100
Tucker, GA 30084

ISBN 978-0-9998210-7-7

CONTENTS

WELCOME

From top leaders to front line workers, engagement matters at all levels. Imagine building a culture where everyone showed up fully engaged and excited about the work…a culture where the potential of every worker was fully unleashed. The competitive advantage you could create would be staggering. The reality is, it can happen.

The path forward begins with a simple definition.

ENGAGEMENT = LEVEL OF CARE.

In this guide, you will discover four cornerstones of engagement that, if applied, will help everyone you lead **CARE** more. The content was created to be applied throughout your organization. Inside you will find best practices, questions, key concepts, and dozens of ideas for action to help you build a culture of engagement. We encourage you to work through each section individually, and with your leaders, so you can apply what you are learning together.

Welcome to the **WIN THE HEART QUICK START GUIDE!**

Mark and Randy

For a full overview of Win the Heart, please reference the Win the Heart Book & Field Guide, available at LeadEveryDay.com.

CONNECTION

SECTION ONE

> When people are connected,
> CARE skyrockets!

Why do some people care more than others? The answer is quite simple: **CONNECTION**. When people are connected to a person or cause, their level of care escalates and so does their engagement. As a leader, your responsibility is to keep people connected to what matters most.

Do you wish your people cared more? If so, you can accelerate engagement levels by encouraging connection to customers, to each other, and to your cause. When people are connected, CARE skyrockets!

CELEBRATE CUSTOMERS

What matters most in your business? Truthfully, without customers, you are out of business. People matter more than profits!

Celebration begins with connection. Making eye contact, sharing a smile, learning a person's name, listening to their story, and adjusting to their feedback are all ways to communicate value. Does your team believe they are there to serve your customers or that the customers are there to serve them?

As the leader, you are responsible for reminding your people to **CELEBRATE CUSTOMERS**. If you truly want to create an environment where customers care about what you have to say or sell, then create a customer-centric business.

PEOPLE MATTER MORE THAN PROFITS

IN GREAT BUSINESSES, CUSTOMERS ARE CELEBRATED NOT TOLERATED

SATISFIED CUSTOMERS ARE BILLBOARDS FOR YOUR BUSINESS

What are three ways you and your team celebrate customers?

THINGS YOU CAN DO TO CELEBRATE CUSTOMERS

☐ **ATTITUDE OF GRATITUDE**

Choose one customer weekly and celebrate them with a handwritten note from your team along with a gift card to a local ice cream or coffee shop.

DATE COMPLETED: _____

☐ **GET TO KNOW THE "REGULARS"**

Challenge yourself and your team to learn the names of at least two regular customers every week.

DATE COMPLETED: _____

☐ SECOND MILE SERVICE

Conduct a quarterly meeting with your leadership team to brainstorm ways you can go the "extra mile" for your customers.

DATE COMPLETED: _____

☐ ABOVE AND BEYOND

Every month, ask your team to offer their input on how you can go "above and beyond" with your customer care.

DATE COMPLETED: _____

☐ SAY THANKS

In every verbal interaction with your customers, ensure you and your team say thank you.

DATE COMPLETED: _____

CREATE BELONGING

People crave belonging. From an early age, we seek out a group, clique, club, or team. While the desire to fit in is universal, without the right environment, connection can be difficult. Wise leaders understand community is cumulative over time, and they work hard to **CREATE BELONGING**—a place where employees feel connected to each other and the customers.

Growing organizations are not built by leaders who merely clock in but by leaders who care 100% of the time. If you want to raise the level of engagement throughout your organization, care for your people and help them connect to each other. A place to belong is a powerful motivator for high performance.

THE DESIRE TO FIT INTO A GROUP IS UNIVERSAL

LEADERS ARE RESPONSIBLE FOR MODELING CARE & CREATING CONNECTION

A PLACE TO BELONG IS A POWERFUL MOTIVATOR FOR HIGH PERFORMANCE

QUESTION TO CONSIDER

How could your team create a greater sense of community?

THINGS YOU CAN DO TO CREATE BELONGING

☐ **NEW TEAM MEMBER MEAL**

Every quarter, schedule a meal out with all new Team Members, paid for by the organization.

DATE COMPLETED: _____

☐ **CHILI COOK OFF**

Invite employees and their families to participate in an annual chili cook off. Provide prizes to the winners.

DATE COMPLETED: _____

☐ STORY TIME

Knowing is the first step in building genuine community. At an upcoming meeting or retreat, ask the attendees to share their personal stories.

DATE COMPLETED: _____

☐ GLAD TO KNOW YOU

Every day, try to learn something about the personal life of a fellow Team Member. Do this for 30 days and see how it transforms your culture.

DATE COMPLETED: _____

☐ BUDGET FOR BELONGING

As you set your budget for next year, be sure to include a line item to fund employee connection activities.

DATE COMPLETED: _____

PERSONALIZE VISION

Leaders not only see the future, they also help others see it too. But it is one thing to cast vision and another to **PERSONALIZE VISION** for every employee. Personalizing the vision can take on many forms. From creating role clarity to providing feedback, leaders convey they are interested in the success and future of their Team Members.

Are your people locked in on contributing to the vision? Have they personalized it to their specific role and responsibility? If you and your leaders will take the time to clarify the vision for every employee, your people will care more, and engagement always energizes effort.

GREAT LEADERS CONSTANTLY PERSONALIZE THE VISION

REMIND PEOPLE OFTEN WHAT THEY DO MATTERS

PEOPLE IN HIGH PERFORMANCE ORGANIZATIONS EMBRACE THE VISION AT EVERY LEVEL

QUESTION TO CONSIDER

How can you connect your direct reports to the vision of the organization?

THINGS YOU CAN DO TO PERSONALIZE VISION

☐ **KNOW THE WHY**

Create an easy to remember statement that explains why you exist as an organization and ensure everyone knows it.

DATE COMPLETED: _____

☐ **ASK THEM**

During your one-on-one evaluations, make sure you ask Team Members what part they played in living out the vision of the company.

DATE COMPLETED: _____

☐ LAST MONTH LOOKBACK

Ask each member of your team to identify the most important thing they did to live out the vision of the organization during the past month.

DATE COMPLETED: _____

☐ POWER OF STORY

Your team needs to know the history of your organization. During orientation and at least twice a year moving forward, highlight the history of the company.

DATE COMPLETED: _____

☐ PHOTO LINE UP

Give all new Team Members an organizational chart with names, photos, and positions of every leader in the organization.

DATE COMPLETED: _____

AFFIRMATION

> Affirmation is the foundation of engagement.

Few things are as important as **AFFIRMATION**. While individual affirmation matters, a culture of affirmation is powerful. Leaders who understand this and work to make people feel validated create an engaged workforce that produces amazing results.

Do your wish your people cared more? If so, don't allow them to wonder whether or not they matter. As the leader, you are the architect of the culture of your organization. Design a place where everyone receives affirmation, and your people will love coming to work.

SHOW APPRECIATION

Plato once wrote, "What is honored in a country is cultivated there." In other words, if you affirm a behavior, it will be repeated. Do you **SHOW APPRECIATION** to your people? Face it, without your team you would not be able to accomplish very much. But there is a difference in having appreciation and showing it to those you lead. Great leaders create an environment of affirmation by showing appreciation.

If your team is struggling to stay engaged, they may not feel valued. Do your team a favor and become a leader who demonstrates appreciation. Remember, genuine appreciation paves the path to greater engagement.

A CULTURE OF GRATITUDE BRINGS OUT THE BEST IN PEOPLE

SECURE LEADERS SHARE CREDIT

APPRECIATION PAVES THE PATH TO GREATER ENGAGEMENT

QUESTION TO CONSIDER

What effect does your gratitude have on your people?

THINGS YOU CAN DO TO SHOW APPRECIATION

☐ **APPRECIATION LANGUAGE**

There are a variety of ways to communicate appreciation. Ask each person on your team to identify what makes them feel appreciated (i.e. words, gifts, notes, etc.), and begin showing individual appreciation.

DATE COMPLETED: _____

☐ **ASK YOUR STAFF**

Ask your team if they feel appreciated by the company and why or why not. Really listen and work to show appreciation using what you learn from your conversations.

DATE COMPLETED: _____

☐ WRITTEN WORDS

Make it a point to handwrite three cards every week expressing your appreciation for your employees.

DATE COMPLETED: _____

☐ APPRECIATION WEEK

Schedule an employee appreciation week at least two times each year. Make each day of appreciation week a special event with a different theme.

DATE COMPLETED: _____

☐ NOT ANOTHER NUMBER

Do one thing each week to make one member of your team feel like more than just another number.

DATE COMPLETED: _____

VALIDATE PEOPLE

"Do I have what it takes?" How about your people? Do you think they ever wonder? They shouldn't. As a leader, one of your greatest opportunities for influence is to assure your people they matter, not just as employees but also as individuals.

The mantle of leadership carries with it a megaphone. What you say and do communicates loudly just how important you believe your people are. If you will work on creating a culture of affirmation where every person is validated, your people will love working for you. Your responsibility is to **VALIDATE PEOPLE**.

**THE LEADER'S WORDS
CARRY THE MOST WEIGHT**

**VALIDATION
CREATES MOTIVATION**

**PEOPLE MUST FEEL VALUED
BY THEIR LEADERS**

QUESTION TO CONSIDER

Who needs your validation
in the next week?

THINGS YOU CAN DO TO VALIDATE PEOPLE

☐ **TALK & LISTEN**

Make it a habit in your conversations to really listen to what others have to say.

DATE COMPLETED: _____

☐ **RESULTS & RELATIONSHIPS**

Don't fall into the trap of only focusing on results. The best leaders value BOTH results AND relationships. Ask those you work with to help you modify your behavior to ensure you don't miss either.

DATE COMPLETED: _____

☐ INVEST FOR GROWTH

Offer at least one opportunity per month for your Team Members to grow. (Think: podcast, article, book, blog or seminar).

DATE COMPLETED: _____

☐ ACKNOWLEDGE EFFORT

At every team meeting, publicly acknowledge individual efforts.

DATE COMPLETED: _____

☐ GIFT CARDS

Purchase a stack of gift cards monthly, and as you catch someone doing something great, give them one.

DATE COMPLETED: _____

FOSTER DREAMS

Do you know the dreams of your people? Leaders who really care for their employees work hard to **FOSTER DREAMS** for everyone on the the team, both inside and outside of work.

The people in your organization carry with them hopes and aspirations for a better tomorrow. When you become aware of what your people really desire, you are positioned to encourage them, remove barriers, and celebrate with them. Lock in on the things important to those you lead, and you will become more important to them. After all, who doesn't admire a leader who makes dreams come true?

IN THE BEST ORGANIZATIONS, PEOPLE ARE ENCOURAGED TO DREAM

GREAT LEADERS CELEBRATE THE DREAMS OF THEIR PEOPLE

PEOPLE WANT TO WORK FOR LEADERS WHO HELP MAKE DREAMS COME TRUE

QUESTION TO CONSIDER

How could your organization become a place where dreams come true?

THINGS YOU CAN DO TO
FOSTER DREAMS

☐ **START SMALL - DREAM BIG**

Encourage every Team Member to have a dream, no matter how small. Once they achieve something small, challenge them to dream big.

DATE COMPLETED: _____

☐ **DREAM TO DEVELOP**

Ensure every Team Member has a development plan focused on what is and what could be. Remind them to keep their dream in mind as they plan.

DATE COMPLETED: _____

☐ SCHOLARSHIP PROGRAM

If you have the financial margin, create a company scholarship program to assist employees in furthering their education.

DATE COMPLETED: _____

☐ 30 MINUTE WALK THRU

Spend 30 minutes a day for the next week walking around and talking to your employees about their dreams, goals, and aspirations.

DATE COMPLETED: _____

☐ BREAKING BARRIERS

Talk with your Team Members about potential barriers between them and their dream. Together, look for ways you can help remove the barriers.

DATE COMPLETED: _____

RESPONSIBILITY

SECTION THREE

> If you only hire a man's hands, you miss the opportunity to win his heart!

Do you want your people to care more? If so, give them more **RESPONSIBILITY**. The sign of a great leader is not the ability to attract followers but rather to grow more leaders. Sharing responsibility is one of the best things you can do to develop your people.

A well-led team is willing to accept responsibility. Give your people the opportunity to share the load, and everyone will benefit—especially you!

DELEGATE DECISIONS

The number of decisions leaders make is endless. The question is, "Why?" Possibly, they don't understand the power of delegating decisions to their team. Leaders who desire for their people to be more responsible empower them to make choices.

Do you remember the first time a leader delegated an important decision to you? Can you recall when a supervisor asked, "What do you think we should do?" How did it make you feel when you knew the outcome might be affected by your opinion? Exhilarated? Energized? Engaged? Your people can feel the same way if you will trust them.

If you want to accelerate the growth of your business, trust your people and **DELEGATE DECISIONS**.

GREAT ORGANIZATIONS EMPOWER DECISION MAKERS AT ALL LEVELS

WEIGH-IN LEADS TO BUY IN

WHEN YOU MAKE THE DECISION, YOU CARE MORE ABOUT THE DECISION

What is one decision you currently need to delegate?

THINGS YOU CAN DO TO DELEGATE DECISIONS

☐ **IT'S YOURS!**

Look at your to-do list and give away one thing each week to a trusted coworker.

DATE COMPLETED: _____

☐ **GIVE IT AWAY**

Choose a project to delegate. Refuse to micromanage or specify methods but be clear on the desired outcomes and any boundaries that exist.

DATE COMPLETED: _____

☐ STRETCH ASSIGNMENTS

Come up with at least three assignments (with appropriate decision-making authority) this month that will stretch a Team Member to perform at a higher level and contribute more to the company.

DATE COMPLETED: _____

☐ DELEGATE UPDATE

Once you delegate a decision, empower and entrust the person to own it. Ask for updates as needed.

DATE COMPLETED: _____

☐ CONFIRM CLARITY

Every time you delegate a big decision, follow up with written communication to ensure the expectations are clear.

DATE COMPLETED: _____

SHARE OWNERSHIP

Hoarding has become a well known phenomenon in our culture. Leaders can become hoarders by owning every decision, outcome, and initiative.

Ultimately, leaders carry the weight of responsibility for everything they lead. High performance leaders understand the power of shared ownership, and their results flourish.

The people around you are willing to help you carry the load if you are willing to **SHARE OWNERSHIP**. Is it time for you to de-clutter your leadership and trust your people?

HIGH PERFORMANCE LEADERS TRUST THEIR PEOPLE ENOUGH TO SHARE OWNERSHIP

SHARING OWNERSHIP GROWS CAPACITY AND ENGAGEMENT

IN GREAT ORGANIZATIONS EVERYONE OWNS SOMETHING, AND EVERYTHING IS OWNED

How well do your people take ownership, and what does that say about your leadership?

THINGS YOU CAN DO TO SHARE OWNERSHIP

EMPOWER SOMEONE

Choose one responsibility this week to give away. Select someone you think is ready for a challenge and empower them. Check back in a week to see how things are going.

DATE COMPLETED: _____

VALUE OF REAL RESPONSIBILITY

Name a real responsibility you can assign this week that will indicate you value a Team Member's contribution to the company.

DATE COMPLETED: _____

☐ OWNERSHIP AUDIT

Take a look at your employee roster. Beside each person's name, make a list of what they own. Does everyone own something?

DATE COMPLETED: _____

☐ YOU SHOULD KEEP THIS

Be slow to accept work from a Team Member. Instead, ask questions such as, "What have you attempted already? What have you learned? What next steps could you take?"

DATE COMPLETED: _____

☐ TEAM FEEDBACK

Create a formal mechanism for your team to offer feedback and input on important decisions.

DATE COMPLETED: _____

ESTABLISH ACCOUNTABILITY

If you need a picture of accountability, look no further than your bathroom scales. They never lie. Those who value fitness don't view the scales as something bad. In fact, they appreciate the power of the accountability. The scales are unemotional. They simply give information that reflects how a person is doing in the areas of exercise and nutrition. Unfortunately, accountability in the workplace is often viewed as negative.

If you want your people to take responsibility for their actions, then give them permission to make progress, and coach them along the way. There is tremendous potential in your organization. Will you give your people a gift and ESTABLISH ACCOUNTABILITY?

ACCOUNTABILITY IMPROVES PERFORMANCE

THE BEST LEADERS CONSISTENTLY GIVE THE GIFT OF ACCOUNTABILITY

ACCOUNTABILITY INCREASES ENGAGEMENT

Who needs to be held accountable for a negative attitude or poor performance?

THINGS YOU CAN DO TO ESTABLISH ACCOUNTABILITY

☐ **ONE ON ONE**

Have an accountability conversation with a different employee at the first of every month for the next year. Agree upon one area where you will be accountable to each other. Report back on progress at the end of the month.

DATE COMPLETED: _____

☐ **THE LAST 10%**

In conversations with your direct reports, commit to sharing the last 10% of the truth. Remember that candid feedback can be a catalyst for growth.

DATE COMPLETED: _____

☐ CLARIFY EXPECTATIONS

When discussing an assignment with your team, always recap what is expected of each individual.

DATE COMPLETED: _____

☐ TRACK THE COMMITMENTS

Make sure your leadership team tracks the commitments Team Members make in order to hold them accountable. Review previous action items every time you meet.

DATE COMPLETED: _____

☐ ON THE 30S

Check in with new Team Members every 30 days for at least three months to review the company mission.

DATE COMPLETED: _____

ENVIRONMENT

SECTION FOUR

> The best leaders create
> an Environment of
> Connection, Affirmation,
> and Responsibility.

Some environments are better than others. Beach or mountains? Sunny or snowy? We all have our preferences. Work environments are no different. **ENVIRONMENT** plays a huge role in whether or not a person cares about their job and stays engaged.

If you are the leader, you are in charge of the environment. Work to create the kind of place you would like to work, and your people will show up every day ready to grow.

PROVIDE SAFETY

Have you ever stood on a hotel balcony overlooking the ocean enjoying the beautiful view? Few would experience the joy without the presence of the balcony rail. The rail provides safety and confidence.

If the level of engagement in your business appears to be low, your people may not feel safe. If you will create a balcony rail of support and **PROVIDE SAFETY** for your people, trust will grow and they will embrace your vision.

FEAR COMES IN ALL SHAPES AND SIZES

THE BEST LEADERS CREATE PSYCHOLOGICAL, CULTURAL, AND PHYSICAL SAFETY FOR THEIR PEOPLE

ENGAGEMENT GROWS WHEN PEOPLE FEEL SAFE

QUESTION TO CONSIDER

What is one area where your organization needs a better safety procedure?

THINGS YOU CAN DO TO PROVIDE SAFETY

☐ **SYSTEMS REVIEW**

Conduct a full review of the systems within your organization to evaluate whether they are enabling or inhibiting employee safety.

DATE COMPLETED: _____

☐ **SAFETY FOR EVERYONE**

Work with your team to identify ten ways Team Members can hold one another accountable for workplace safety. Quickly implement the best ideas.

DATE COMPLETED: _____

☐ GUARD THE TEAM

Evaluate the cultural norms in place to protect your team. Ask yourself: are they clear and well-communicated, and is anything missing?

DATE COMPLETED: _____

☐ SEE SOMETHING & SAY SOMETHING

Ask all staff members to say something if they see something that concerns them from a safety perspective.

DATE COMPLETED: _____

☐ PROTECT THE CULTURE

Ensure you have a written policy in place that states harassment of any kind is not permitted, and always offer a clear line of communication to report it.

DATE COMPLETED: _____

EQUIP FOR SUCCESS

The right tools can make a hard task not only doable, but enjoyable. Have you ever attempted a do-it-yourself project when you didn't have the tools needed to succeed? Frustrating, to say the least. A task at work is no different. One of the ways you can create a better environment for your people is to equip them for success.

Don't ask people to do a job they are not prepared to do. Make it a habit to **EQUIP FOR SUCCESS,** and your people will not only enjoy the work, they will do a better job.

WITHOUT THE PROPER SKILLS, WORK BECOMES DRUDGERY

EVERYONE DESERVES CLEAR EXPECTATIONS

WITHOUT THE REQUISITE TRAINING, HIGH LEVELS OF ENGAGEMENT ARE IMPOSSIBLE

QUESTION TO CONSIDER

What is one thing you can do to equip your team this next month?

THINGS YOU CAN DO TO EQUIP FOR SUCCESS

☐ **DEVELOPMENT PLAN**

Ensure all Team Members have a development plan in place that clearly identifies areas of targeted growth.

DATE COMPLETED: _____

☐ **BASIC TRAINING**

Provide every employee with basic training for their current role.

DATE COMPLETED: _____

☐ **TRAINING BUDDY**

Assign a training buddy to each new employee. Ask the veteran to support the new hire until fully trained for current position.

DATE COMPLETED: _____

☐ **SKILL GAPS**

Work with each Team Member individually to identify any skill gaps that need to be addressed. Create a plan and get started.

DATE COMPLETED: _____

☐ **THE STANDARDS**

In order for your company to reach its full potential and your people to be fully engaged, everyone must know what is expected of them. Meet with every Team Member in the next 30 days to clarify the standards for their role.

DATE COMPLETED: _____

LISTEN & RESPOND

Are you a good listener? There aren't many things better than being heard. If you **LISTEN & RESPOND** to your people, the environment moves from good to great.

The ability to listen well is a skill. How much do you work on it? The best leaders learn when to speak and when to stay silent.

If you really want to create a great environment for those you lead, make sure you build in time to listen to your people and respond appropriately.

LISTENING COMMUNICATES CARE

....

THE PEOPLE CLOSEST TO THE PROBLEM ARE CLOSEST TO THE SOLUTION

....

WISE LEADERS SEEK INPUT, THEN RESPOND QUICKLY

How well do you listen and respond
to your Team Members?

THINGS YOU CAN DO TO LISTEN & RESPOND

☐ **STOP, LOOK, LISTEN, RESPOND**

When a Team Member shares a concern, stop what you are doing, look at them, listen to them, and respond as needed.

DATE COMPLETED: _____

☐ **BAD APPLES**

If you consistently hear of an employee bringing the team down, consider a replacement. Review your team quarterly to ensure everyone is still an asset to the organization.

DATE COMPLETED: _____

☐ MONITOR MORALE

Survey your employees to monitor morale. Make improvements based on their feedback.

DATE COMPLETED: _____

☐ DON'T INTERRUPT

Work on creating the habit of not interrupting in all of your conversations. Jot a checkmark on a piece of paper every time you do. Make zero interruptions your daily goal.

DATE COMPLETED: _____

☐ IT STARTS AT THE TOP

Offer your Team Members the opportunity to schedule an appointment with you. Always listen first and then respond accordingly.

DATE COMPLETED: _____

RESOURCES FOR THE LEADER'S JOURNEY

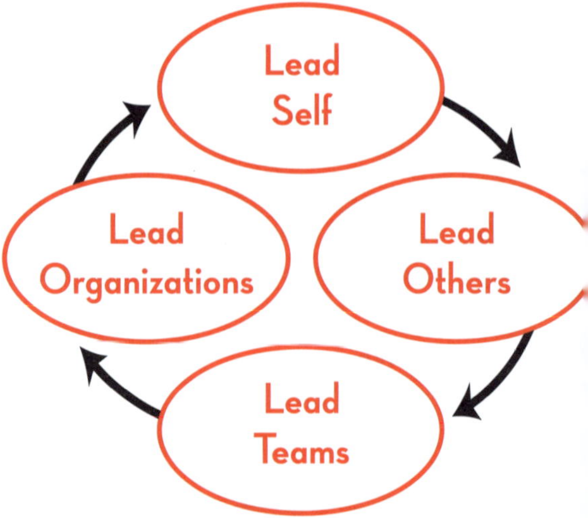
Lead Self
Lead Others
Lead Teams
Lead Organizations

InteGREAT App

CHESS
CHECKERS

The InteGREAT Leadership app is **FREE** on the App Store. Additional resources at: **INTEGREATLEADERSHIP.COM**

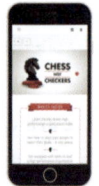